Read ███████ spond

J/BUR

SECTION 3
Shared reading

SECTION 4
Plot, character and setting

SECTION 5
Talk about it

SECTION 6
Get writing

SECTION 7
Assessment

Read & Respond

Ages 7–11

Authors: Sarah Snashall and Huw Thomas

Development Editor: Marion Archer

Editor: Margaret Eaton

Assistant Editor: Sarah Sodhi

Series Designer: Anna Oliwa

Designer: Anna Oliwa

Cover Image: Robin Lawrie

Illustrations: Jon Mitchell

Text © 2011, Sarah Snashall and Huw Thomas © 2011, Scholastic Ltd

Designed using Adobe InDesign

Published by Scholastic Ltd,
Book End, Range Road, Witney,
Oxfordshire OX29 0YD
www.scholastic.co.uk

Printed by Bell & Bain
1 2 3 4 5 6 7 8 9   1 2 3 4 5 6 7 8 9 0

British Library Cataloguing-in-Publication Data
A catalogue record for this book is available from
the British Library.
ISBN 978-1407-12628-9

Acknowledgements
The publishers gratefully acknowledge permission to reproduce the following copyright material: **Puffin Books** for the use of the cover from *The Secret Garden* by Frances Hodgson Burnett. Every effort has been made to trace copyright holders for the works reproduced in this book, and the publishers apologise for any inadvertent omissions.

The Secret Garden

About the book

Like many of Frances Hodgson Burnett's stories, *The Secret Garden* is a story about an outsider and her struggle to belong. Coming from the exotic but scary setting of India, Mary arrives in England and her search for happiness and a loving and secure future is symbolised by her search for a secret garden. When she finds it, the garden symbolises and becomes the cause of new life and rejuvenation. Having spent most of her life abroad, it is Frances's early memories of the English moors and Yorkshire family life that create the setting for the book.

Mary is joined on her emotional journey by Colin, another broken and unloved child. When Colin decides that he wants to live and is taken into the garden, his body becomes strong through 'magic' (or exercise and good food!). Frances was interested in a form of Christian spriritualism and believed that the mind can affect the body.

About the author

Frances Eliza Hodgson was born on 24 November 1849 in Cheetham Hill, Manchester. Her father died when she was very young and her mother and her five children were forced to sell their home and move in with relatives in a poor neighbourhood. Frances's grandmother taught her to read and told her stories; Frances in turn wrote for the family and herself. When Frances was 16 they emigrated to America to join Frances's uncle, but by the time they arrived, his business had failed and the family were thrown into poverty. Frances started to write professionally to support the family. She published her first story aged 18 and supported herself through writing for the rest of her life.

Frances married a neighbour, Swan Burnett, in 1873. They moved to Paris and then to Washington DC. She had two sons, Lionel and Vivian. She loved her sons dearly and delighted in dressing them up in velvet and lace and curling their long hair. Having written for adults until this time, her first children's book, *Little Lord Fauntleroy*, was published in 1886. It was the *Harry Potter* of its day and created a fashion for lace and velvet and *Little Lord Fauntleroy* merchandising.

Frances travelled quite frequently between America, France, Italy and England. She continued to support her family through her writing, including stage versions of her books. She divorced Swan Burnett in 1898 and remarried two years later. She lived for a while in Maytham Hall, Kent – an old manor with a walled rose garden, where she enjoyed writing outside and tending to the plants (this garden is in part the inspiration for the storyline in *The Secret Garden*). Frances' second marriage did not last long and she moved back to New York where her son Vivian had a publishing business. She continued to write children's books, including *A Little Princess* in 1905 and *The Secret Garden* in 1911. Frances died on 29 October 1924, aged 74.

Facts and figures

First published by Frederick A Stokes, New York, in 1911.
First published by Puffin Books in 1951.
BBC audiobook published in 2006.
The Secret Garden has also been adapted into several film versions, TV serials and stage productions.

Guided reading

Chapters 1 to 3

The Secret Garden has a very dramatic opening – and quite an unexpected one for a children's book. More happens here than in the rest of the book put together. Ask: *How do we respond to Mary?* Discuss with the class how she is portrayed (rude and self-centred, heartless and unfriendly). Are the children surprised to find the main character of the book so unpleasant? Is that usual? Talk sensitively about Mary's attitude to the servants in the house.

Read to the end of Chapter 3, then skim back through the previous pages with a more sympathetic eye. Point out Mr Crawford's comment in Chapter 2, *'Perhaps if her mother…'* Ask: *Is Mary unlovable because she's unloved?* Reflect on the way she was abandoned in the bungalow and how she is treated in the clergyman's home. Do the children blame Mary?

How do the children respond to comments about Mary's appearance? Comments on appearance and superficial judgement are a feature of the book – her looks are used as a way to reflect on her wellbeing and character. What do the children think about Frances Hodgson-Burnett's portrayal of Mr Craven as a hunchback? Is this a problem and insensitive, or does it just give Mr Craven a reason to worry about his son?

Re-read the final pages of Chapter 3 relating to Mary's arrival at Misselthwaite Manor. Encourage the children to reflect on how different this is from India, how far Mary has travelled and how she might feel arriving at night at this gloomy place, owned by a bad-tempered hunchback. Recall all the things that have happened to her up to this point. Ask the children to provide cases for and against her feeling so 'contrary'.

Make a list of how we have felt about Mary so far. Stress the range of emotions and explain that it is the author's skill that allows us to feel both revulsion and sorrow for Mary at the same time.

Chapters 4 to 6

Setting is hugely important in *The Secret Garden* and a major part of this is the moor itself. Although no scenes actually take place on it, it's talked about on many occasions. What do the children know about moors? Does the mental image of a moor conjure up positive or negative thoughts? Bring in the children's general responses to the outdoors. In *The Secret Garden*, the moor, like the house itself, is set up to be somewhere scary that turns out to be something wonderful in the end.

Read Chapter 4 and discuss the role of servants in the story. Place the story in its historical context. Mary's treatment of the servants is one way that we see her growing sense of others and how to treat them. Compare how Martha and Mary's Ayah respond to Mary. Remind the children about the mixed attitudes we have towards Mary at the start and apply this to Mary's imperious question *'Who is going to dress me?'* (She acts like a queen, but no one has taught her to dress herself.) Look at the phrase *'It was the custom'*. Ask: *Is Mary bad to expect to be dressed?*

In Chapter 4 Mary meets the robin and Ben Weatherstaff, who are both important in Mary's development – the robin because it is the first creature to like her and Ben because Mary sees his crabby nature and understands that she is also like that.

Before moving on to Chapter 5, discuss loneliness with the children. How do they respond to being lonely? As they read Chapters 5 and 6, ask them to focus on the locations: the moor, the gardens in winter, the house at night (with the noise of crying). What feelings are elicited by the descriptions of these locations? How do they affect readers' attitudes towards Mary? (We feel sorry for her and she seems very alone in a desolate place.)

Chapters 7 to 9

As you read the opening of Chapter 7, ask the children if they can detect the good things that are happening. Point to the title of the chapter and predict what is going to happen. Can they see that this is a turning point in the story – where the miserable opening ends and the rest of the story starts?

Guided reading

Reflect together on how Mary acts around Martha; discuss how this is probably her first 'normal' relationship. Read the conversation where Mary admits she doesn't like herself and gather responses. How do the children think that this might change?

Read through to the end of Chapter 8 and look at the process of entering the garden (locating the garden, finding the key and finding the door). Are the children surprised at how early in the book Mary gets into the garden? Predict what else might need to happen before the end (hopefully they will remember the crying in the night and see this as a mystery that needs to be solved).

Read Chapter 9. How is the process of being in the garden gradually unfolded? (First Mary hardly dares to move because it feels enchanted, then she walks slowly, finally she starts working and becomes relaxed and naturally knows how to help the bulbs.) Revisit the first three pages of the book and look again at how unpleasant and pitiful she was (compare Mary pretending to garden in Chapter 1 with her real garden now). Ask: *How are our responses to Mary changing?* (We probably like her better and no longer feel so sorry for her.)

Chapters 10 to 12

Re-read Martha's letter to Dickon in Chapter 9. Ask: *What do we expect Dickon to be like?* Read Chapter 10, then revisit Mary's conversation with Dickon and talk about his effect on her. Look at Mary's conversation with Ben Weatherstaff – together unpick the mystery of the young lady (Mr Craven's wife) and her garden. Do the children realise that Ben has been into the secret garden and pruned the roses?

Mary is now going to meet the ominous Mr Craven: what do the children expect from this? Read to the end of Chapter 12. Carefully re-read the conversation, picking out the way Mary cleverly secures his permission to work in the secret garden. Note the way he responds to her interest in gardening. Can the children think how he might respond in the future?

Chapters 13 and 15

Before reading Chapter 13, discuss the crying that Mary has heard in the night. What might it be? Now read to the end of Chapter 14. Were any of the children's predictions correct? Look at how Mary talks about the garden – guarding her words with *think* and *might*. Was it similar to the conversation with Mr Craven or Dickon? Talk about how each conversation differs.

Follow the story that Colin tells of his life. What do we make of it? Make the connections between Mary and Colin's lives and how their experiences have shaped their characters. Knowing what has happened to Mary, what do the children predict will happen to Colin? Read Chapter 15 and encourage the children to look at how Mary relates to Colin and Dickon. Invite them to pick out some of the main differences, finding lines in the text that reveal these differences.

Chapters 16 to 20

Read Chapters 16 and 17 and revisit Colin's life. How is he treated by the staff? Ask: *Why could Mary shout back at him?* (Because she's not a member of staff and she doesn't care what Colin thinks of her.) Discuss the importance of Mary finally shocking Colin into facing up to his fears and deciding to get on with his life.

Read Chapter 18 and ask the children to pick out how Mary grows in her relationship with Colin. What is achieved by the end of this chapter? (Mary has shown her trust in Colin.) Ask: *Why is this trust so important?* (It shows how both Mary and Colin are beginning to form proper relationships.) *How might Mary telling Colin about the garden move the plot on?* (Colin will want to go outside and see it.) *How might it all go wrong?*

Read Chapter 20 and talk about how others view Colin: his father, the staff, Dr Craven. Re-read Dickon's visit and then the invasion of animals and fresh air into the sick room. Savour the description. Read together what Colin says at each point and discuss what he is thinking. Ask: *What is the experience doing for Colin?*

Guided reading

Chapters 21 to 23

Ask the children what, so far, they think has been the single most important chapter in the book. (Chapter 8 where Mary enters the garden? Chapter 13 where she meets Colin?) Read Chapter 21, which is one of the most crucial chapters in the book. As they read, display the words 'tree', 'robin', 'Ben' and 'chair' on the board. Ask the children to note how these elements feature and how they are abandoned. At the end of the chapter, pause and discuss the key points.

Read Chapters 22 and 23 and discuss the notion of magic in the book. Do the children think that magic takes place? Ask: *What do we usually mean by 'magic'?*

Chapters 24 to 27

Talk about Mrs Sowerby and her role in the story. (Model mother, wise woman and practical help.) Re-read her conversation with Dickon. Do the children agree with her comment that Mary coming to the house has been *'th' makin' o' her an' th' savin' o' him'*?

Read to the end of Chapter 26. This final section of the book allows time for Colin to get better and the garden to blossom. Mrs Sowerby remains a figure of the perfect mother, but at the end of this chapter she says something very special to Colin – that his mother is watching him in the garden. In Chapter 27 she does something just as important, but more practical – she writes to Colin's father encouraging him to come home. What do the children think Mr Craven will expect and what will he find? Read to the end of Chapter 27 and enjoy the happy ending.

So the book, which starts with the death of Mary's parents, ends with the return of Colin's father and her guardian.

Shared reading

Extract 1

● Extract 1 is taken from Chapter 2. Talk about the ironic first line. How might a house *with a hundred rooms nearly all shut up* lend itself to a story?

● Read through the first paragraph and circle the descriptive words and phrases (*shut up, edge of a moor, crooked, grey slanting lines* and so on). What feelings do they conjure up?

● Focus on the mystery surrounding the pretty wife – who might this be? Where has she gone and how might this change the house? (It might be a sad place to live.)

● Ask: *What does the second paragraph tell us about Mrs Medlock?* (That she's quite unfeeling and strict; that her loyalties lie with Mr Craven.) *What might we expect from her?* (Practical rather than loving treatment.)

● Relive the train journey through Mary's eyes. Number from 1 to 5 the five things that take Mary from feeling sad to feeling thoroughly miserable. Ask: *What is life going to be like at this place?*

Extract 2

● Display Extract 2 (from Chapter 10), hiding everything apart from the opening line. Ask: *What sort of a place can a secret garden be? What are the joys of it being secret, and the risks?*

● Now reveal the rest of the passage and focus on how Mary is described. In what way is she like the garden? (She is also becoming healthy and strong.) How is her life different from what we might have predicted from Extract 1?

● Talk about Mary's thoughts about fairy tales. Can the children think of fairy stories that feature secret places, spells and so on? Point out the similarity to a storybook setting of a manor with a hundred locked rooms.

● What do they think about Mary's comments about those who went to sleep for a hundred years? Has she been asleep in some way all her life? Underline *in fact, she was becoming wider awake every day*. In what way can a person be wider awake?

● Look at the personification of the bulbs. Can the children explain the meaning of this reference? (Perhaps this shows how Mary is now beginning to think of something other than herself; perhaps it is the author's way of showing how the garden is responding to Mary's care.)

● Reflect on the final paragraph. How does this fit with how Mary is changing? (She is enjoying having a purpose for the first time; she is part play-acting – she still half feels that she's living in a fairy tale or play.)

Extract 3

● Extract 3 is taken from Chapter 20. Read the text together; invite different children to speak the lines of Colin and Mary with appropriate expression. How well can they capture the excitement of the two characters?

● Talk about how much of the story has been leading to this point. Draw attention to the way in which the author makes it as dramatic as possible through Mary's commentary, pointing out where each of the events took place.

● Discuss how the plot has been developed with each event building on the former: first Mary locates the garden, then she locates the key, and finally she locates the door.

● Discuss Colin's reaction to Mary's commentary. Look at what he says, as well as the way he says it, and how it builds up the reader's expectations.

● Focus on the last line of the extract. Invite the children to explain Colin's feelings at this point.

Extract 1

It sounded like something in a book, and it did not make Mary feel cheerful. A house with a hundred rooms, nearly all shut up and with their doors locked – a house on the edge of a moor – whatsoever a moor was – sounded dreary. A man with a crooked back who shut himself up also! She stared out of the window with her lips pinched together, and it seemed quite natural that the rain should have begun to pour down in grey slanting lines and splash and stream down the window-panes. If the pretty wife had been alive, she might have made things cheerful by being something like her own mother and by running in and out and going to parties as she had done in frocks 'full of lace'. But she was not there any more.

'You needn't expect to see him, because ten to one you won't,' said Mrs Medlock. 'And you mustn't expect that there will be people to talk to you. You'll have to play about and look after yourself. You'll be told what rooms you can go into and what rooms you're to keep out of. There's gardens enough. But when you're in the house don't go wandering and poking about. Mr Craven won't have it.'

'I shall not want to go poking about,' said sour little Mary; and just as suddenly as she had begun to be rather sorry for Mr Archibald Craven, she began to cease to be sorry and to think he was unpleasant enough to deserve all that had happened to him.

And she turned her face towards the streaming panes of the window of the railway carriage and gazed out at the grey rain-storm which looked as if it would go on for ever and ever. She watched it so long and steadily that the greyness grew heavier and heavier before her eyes and she fell asleep.

Text by Frances Hodgson Burnett.

Extract 2

The sun shone down for nearly a week on the secret garden. The Secret Garden was what Mary called it when she was thinking of it. She liked the name, and she liked still more the feeling that when its beautiful old walls shut her in, no one knew where she was. It seemed almost like being shut out of the world in some fairy place. The few books she had read and liked had been fairy-story books, and she had read of secret gardens in some of the stories. Sometimes people went to sleep in them for a hundred years, which she had thought must be rather stupid. She had no intention of going to sleep, and, in fact, she was becoming wider awake every day which passed at Misselthwaite. She was beginning to like to be out of doors; she no longer hated the wind, but enjoyed it. She could run faster, and longer, and she could skip up to a hundred. The bulbs in the secret garden must have been much astonished. Such nice clear spaces were made round them that they had all the breathing space they wanted, and really, if Mistress Mary had known it, they began to cheer up under the dark earth and work tremendously. The sun could get at them and warm them, and when the rain came down it could reach them at once, so they began to feel very much alive.

Mary was an odd, determined little person, and, now she had something interesting to be determined about, she was very much absorbed indeed. She worked and dug and pulled up weeds steadily, only becoming more pleased with her work every hour instead of tiring of it. It seemed to her like a fascinating sort of play.

Text by Frances Hodgson Burnett.

Extract 3

'This is it,' breathed Mary. 'This is where I used to walk up and down and wonder and wonder.'

'Is it?' cried Colin, and his eyes began to search the ivy with eager curiousness. 'But I can see nothing,' he whispered. 'There is no door.'

'That's what I thought,' said Mary.

Then there was a lovely, breathless silence and the chair wheeled on.

'That is the garden where Ben Weatherstaff works,' said Mary.

'Is it?' said Colin.

A few yards more and Mary whispered again.

'This is where the robin flew over the wall,' she said.

'Is it?' cried Colin. 'Oh! I wish he'd come again!'

'And that,' said Mary with solemn delight, pointing under a big lilac bush, 'is where he perched on the little heap of earth and showed me the key.'

Then Colin sat up.

'Where? Where? There?' he cried, and his eyes were as big as the wolf's in Red Riding Hood, when Red Riding Hood felt called upon to remark on them. Dickon stood still and the wheeled-chair stopped.

'And this,' said Mary, stepping on to the bed close to the ivy, 'is where I went to talk to him when he chirped at me from the top of the wall. And this is the ivy the wind blew back,' and she took hold of the hanging green curtain.

'Oh! is it –' gasped Colin.

'And here is the handle, and here is the door. Dickon, push him in – push him in quickly!'

Text by Frances Hodgson Burnett.

Plot, character and setting

Questions

> **Objective:** To sustain engagement with longer texts, using different techniques to make the text come alive.
> **What you need:** Copies of *The Secret Garden*, supply of A6 paper slips, string and clothes pegs.

What to do

● Read up to Chapter 6 before carry out this activity.
● Organise the children into pairs. Provide them with a supply of A6 (quarter of A4) paper slips.
● *The Secret Garden* has an air of mystery throughout it. Explain that this means that the reader will have lots of questions that need to be resolved by the end of the book.
● Challenge the children to devise as many questions about the plot and characters as possible. For example: 'Where is the garden?', 'Who was crying?', 'Who used to live in these rooms?', 'What will happen when…?'

● When the children have completed this task, gather all their questions together and read them aloud to the class (removing any duplicates). Can they answer any of them?
● Using the pegs place the questions on a string across the classroom. As you read further through the book revisit the questions, as they are answered take them down, replacing them with new questions as the plot unfolds (for example, 'Is Colin really ill?'). Are there any questions left unanswered at the end of the book?

> **Differentiation**
> **For older/more confident learners:** Ask the children to repeat this activity with one of their own writing stories. Do they notice how adding mystery to any story can make it more interesting to read?
> **For younger/less confident learners:** Provide focus by asking the children to write one question about Mary, one about the mysterious crying and one about the garden.

What we feel about Mary

> **Objective:** To understand underlying themes, causes and points of view.
> **What you need:** Copies of *The Secret Garden*, photocopiable page 15 and scissors.
> **Cross-curricular link:** PSHE.

What to do

● Organise the children to work in groups of three. Ask the groups to think back over the book and choose three significant points in the story. (For example: Mary's arrival at Misselthwaite Manor, when Mary finds the garden, Colin's first trip outside.) Remind the children to listen to each other and to come to a group decision about their three choices.
● Provide each group with photocopiable page 15. Having decided on their three choices, ask the children to fill in the table for the events they have chosen. (Encourage them to all work

together on each event rather than taking one each.)
● Challenge the children to review the book and add further details to explain their thoughts about each event.
● When they have done this, ask them to cut out the three events and work as a whole class to put all the events into the correct order as they appear in the book. Where the same events have been covered by different groups, compare the children's answers.

> **Differentiation**
> **For older/more confident learners:** Invite the children to comment on how their feelings about Mary change between the events. Steer them towards events that no one else has chosen.
> **For younger/less confident learners:** Ask the children to cover just one or two events as appropriate.

Plot, character and setting

Colin's progress

Objective: To sustain engagement with longer texts, using different techniques to make the text come alive.
What you need: Copies of *The Secret Garden*, photocopiable page 16 and scissors.

What to do
● Although Colin does not do a great deal in *The Secret Garden*, it is his progress that forms the motivation for the plot in the second half of the book.
● Provide each child with photocopiable page 16. Ask the children to cut out the events and to put them in order without looking at the book. Some are clear but others, such as 'Spring has come', could fall in a number of places.

● Ask: *Do the events in some of the boxes cause events mentioned in other boxes?*
● Finally, confirm the correct order of the events by skimming through *The Secret Garden* with the class.
● Conclude by discussing why Colin is the way he is with reference to his father, his uncle, and the staff.

Differentiation
For older/more confident learners: Ask the children to add annotations to the events on the slips of paper to provide details of what happened at each particular point.
For younger/less confident learners: Ask the children to work only with the six events covered in the left-hand column of the photocopiable sheet.

Causal links

Objective: To understand underlying themes, causes and points of view.
What you need: Copies of *The Secret Garden* and photocopiable page 17.
Cross-curricular link: History.

What to do
● Ask the children to think of key points in their lives or the lives of their family – moving house, meeting friends for the first time, choosing a school or having a new sibling. How would things have worked out differently if they had taken a different course?
● Ask the children to list crucial points in *The Secret Garden*. Talk about which events could have gone differently. For example, what if Mr Craven hadn't gone away, or buried the key?
● Organise the children to work in pairs. Give each pair photocopiable page 17 (preferably enlarged to A3). The sheet lists alternative events to what happens in the story and invites the children to contemplate what impact they would have had.

● Ask the children to examine each event in turn. Challenge them to first remember what did happen in the story and the result of this event (Mary found the key or found Colin), and from this make the link to what would not have happened without this occuring. The children should then think about what might have happened instead.
● Encourage the children to think about events both in the short and long term. For example, if Mary had not found Colin when she did, she might have eventually met him but by then it would have been too late for him to get better.
● Discuss all the different scenarios and ensure that the children have understood the causal link between the various events in the plot.

Differentiation
For older/more confident learners: Encourage the children to follow through one or two of the scenarios more fully.
For younger/less confident learners: Ask the children to focus only on the robin and the crying in the night.

Plot, character and setting

Who and where?

Objective: To compare the usefulness of techniques such as visualisation, prediction and empathy in exploring the meaning of texts.
What you need: Copies of *The Secret Garden*, photocopiable page 18, scissors, paper and glue.

What to do
● Discuss with the class the various settings featured in *The Secret Garden* and make a list: Mary's parents' bungalow, the clergyman's house, the boat, the train, the manor, and so on. Circle the main settings: the secret garden and Colin's room.
● Next, draw up a list of the main characters.
● Talk about the fact that so much of the plot of *The Secret Garden* centres around conversations between two people only. Tell the children to imagine new meetings and conversations between two characters.

● Provide pairs of children with photocopiable page 18. Invite them to look at different combinations of two characters and one setting and to discuss and make notes on what the characters might say. For example, Mary and Colin meet at night in Colin's room – but who else might meet Colin there? When do they meet and what do they say?
● Invite the children to select their most successful combinations of characters and settings and to share the made-up conversations with the rest of the class.

Differentiation
For older/more confident learners: Encourage the children to reflect on how the settings contribute to the events in the story.
For younger/less confident learners: Allow the children to focus on just four settings and four characters.

First meetings

Objective: To make notes on and use evidence from across a text to explain events or ideas.
What you need: Copies of *The Secret Garden* and writing materials.

What to do
● Talk with the class about all the first meetings that take place in the book. Many of these are built up with anticipation. Ask the children to think of three first meetings (Mary and Martha; Mary and Colin; Mary and Dickon; Dickon and Colin; and so on) and to re-read the relevant passages.
● Invite the children to choose one meeting and ask: *Was it good? Was it surprising? How did the characters react to each other?* Dickon's meeting with Colin is magical for Colin; Mary's meetings with Martha and with Mr Craven both go surprisingly well; Colin is not as scary as Mary fears. It is a feature of the book that the meetings

between characters are subtly different from what may be expected.
● Encourage the children to make notes about the selected meeting and then take turns to present their thoughts to the class. They should take on board any interesting comments offered by their audience.
● Now ask the children to write a report about the meeting with subheadings such as 'Expectations', 'The meeting' and 'Moving forward' (how the relationship between the characters works out).

Differentiation
For older/more confident learners: Ask the children to add an extra paragraph to their report describing the significance of the meeting to the plot.
For younger/less confident learners: Allow the children to focus only on the expectations and the meeting when they write their report.

Plot, character and setting

Rate my character

Objective: To understand underlying themes, causes and points of view.
What you need: Copies of *The Secret Garden*, strips of paper and writing material.
Cross-curricular link: PSHE.

What to do
● *The Secret Garden* evokes complex responses to its complex characters. It's easy to like Dickon, but is he too blandly lovely compared to feisty Mary? Is Mr Craven likeable? Do we ever like Colin, even at the end? (I don't.) Explain that in this activity the children are going to rate the characters in terms of likeability.
● Make a list of the main characters: Mary, Martha, Ben Weatherstaff, Dickon, Colin, Mr Craven, Dr Craven, Mrs Sowerby, Mrs Medlock. Invite a volunteer to order the characters, from their favourite to their least favourite.
● Invite other volunteers to re-order the list according to their preference, explaining their reasons. Encourage utter disagreement.

● Which two characters have moved about the most in the children's lists? (Probably Mary and Colin.) Ask the children to work in pairs to chart their feelings about these two characters on two separate long strips of paper. (Mary: we dislike her → family dies; she moves: we feel sorry for her → rude to Martha: we dislike her → finds the robin and garden: we become interested → works on the garden: we want her to succeed → shouts at Colin: we like her feistiness → she helps Colin: we like her…).
● Put the two strips side by side and see how our responses are linked: when Colin is most hateful, Mary becomes feisty rather than petulant. When Mary is most strong, Colin learns to behave. Explain to the children that Mary and Colin save each other.

Differentiation
For older/more confident learners: Challenge the children to create a similar charts for Mr Craven.
For younger/less confident learners: Ask the children to focus only on their feelings about Mary.

Character point of view

Objective: To infer writers' perspectives from what is written and from what is implied.
What you need: Copies of *The Secret Garden*.

What to do
● Organise the children to work in groups of three and to sit in a circle facing each other. Ask them each to take on the role of one of the main characters in the story (they each need to be someone different).
● Tell the children that Mary has just arrived at Misselthwaite. In role, encourage the children to take turns to say what they think of each other. (Remind them that Colin won't know about Mary, or Mary about him, but everyone else will; remind them also that Mary and Colin are pretty indifferent to others at the beginning.)

● Now leap to the midpoint in the story and repeat the activity. How do the characters feel about each other now? Have their feelings changed?
● Repeat the activity again for the end of the story.
● If there is sufficient time, ask the children to form completely new groups of three. Ensure they each take on a new role and repeat the whole activity.

Differentiation
For older/more confident learners: Encourage the children to discuss why their character thinks this way. Have a conversation between the characters.
For younger/less confident learners: Invite the children to work in pairs and look at what Martha and Mary, or Colin and Mary, think of each other.

What we feel about Mary

● Choose three important events in *The Secret Garden*. What do you think about Mary at each of these points?

What do you think about…	Event 1:	Event 2:	Event 3:
…how Mary is described?			
…what Mary says?			
…the things Mary does?			
…how Mary is with other people?			

Colin's progress

● Cut out the events and put them in the order in which they occur in *The Secret Garden.*

Colin runs to his father.	Colin goes outside.
Colin says, 'I shall get well.'	Colin meets Dickon.
Mary looks at Colin's back.	Mary promises Colin he can meet Dickon.
Mary argues with Colin.	Mary tells Colin she has found the garden.
Colin enters the garden.	Spring has come.
Colin cries in the night.	The doctor visits.

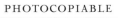

Causal links

● How would things have been different if the following events had occurred?

Events	What would not have happened?	What might have happened instead?
Mary had been happy in her new home.		
Martha had not been nice to Mary.		
The robin had not flown to Mary and Ben.		
Mary had not heard the crying in the night.		
Mary had not met Dickon.		

Who and where?

● Cut out the cards and create new meetings in different settings.

Settings

Mary's room	Ben's garden
The moor	The secret garden
Colin's room	Mr Craven's room

Characters

Colin		Mr Craven	
Dr Craven		Mrs Medlock	
Dickon		Mary	

Illustrations © 2011, Jon Mitchell (Beehive Illustration).

READ & RESPOND: Activities based on The Secret Garden

Talk about it

A bit of earth

> **Objective:** To perform a scripted scene making use of dramatic conventions.
> **What you need:** Copies of *The Secret Garden* and photocopiable page 22.
> **Cross-curricular link:** Drama.

What to do

● Hand out copies of photocopiable page 22. Explain that this is a playscript version of the meeting between Mary and Mr Craven in Chapter 12. After recalling where this comes in the story (Mary has already found the secret garden and has begun to work outside), ask the children to read the playscript with a partner.

● After the pairs have read through the script a couple of times, ask them to talk about their readings. What tone did they use? Did they bring their knowledge of Mary to the scene? Did they follow the stage directions and did this change how they acted?

● Ask the children to make suggestions as to why the characters behave as they do. (Mr Craven turns away from Mary because he's not interested in her until he becomes engaged in what she says; he covers his eyes when he thinks of his wife; he smiles when Mary finally wins him over.)

● Challenge the pairs to gradually learn the playscript by heart, practising bits at a time. Explain that it doesn't need to be word perfect but that they do need to capture the essence of the conversation.

> **Differentiation**
> **For older/more confident learners:** Encourage the children to develop the scene either through improvisation or from gathering extra lines from the book.
> **For younger/less confident learners:** Ask the children to practise a version of the scene using the script.

Who said what?

> **Objective:** To understand underlying themes, causes and points of view.
> **What you need:** Copies of *The Secret Garden*, photocopiable page 23, scissors and writing materials.
> **Cross-curricular link:** History.

What to do

● Provide groups of three children with photocopiable page 23.

● Tell the children to take turns to read out the quotes. Can the group agree on who said it?

● Invite the children to discuss when each quote was said, and why. Who was the character talking to? Challenge them to listen to each other and agree on an answer.

● Now ask the children to locate the quotation in their copies of *The Secret Garden*. Tell them to read the surrounding passage (changing their opinion if necessary) and to write their answers in the table.

● As a whole class, discuss the children's answers (particularly the responses to why the quote was said). Hopefully the children will come up with a range of different suggestions. Talk together about the importance of each quotation in the story and how it feeds into the development of the plot.

> **Differentiation**
> **For older/more confident learners:** Challenge the children to find more quotations in the book that they can use to quiz other children.
> **For younger/less confident learners:** Let the children use a copy of the book during their discussion to help them complete the table.

Talk about it

Hysterical!

Objective: To reflect on how working in role helps to explore complex issues.
What you need: Copies of *The Secret Garden*, photocopiable page 24 and scissors.
Cross-curricular link: Drama.

What to do

● Provide groups of four children with photocopiable page 24. Explain that all the words/phrases on the sheet come from the description of Colin's tantrum and Mary's scolding of him for it in Chapter 17. Ask the children to cut out all of the boxes and to place them face down on the table.
● Encourage the children to try to shed their inhibitions while they undertake this activity.
● Ask them to take it in turns to turn over one of the cards and model how they might say something in the manner specified on their chosen card. Explain that they might like to say the sort of things that children would be likely to say during a tantrum. For example: 'It's not fair', 'You don't like me', 'Leave me alone' and so on.
● Once everyone has taken their turn, ask the groups to locate the tantrum in Chapter 17 (it's about two pages in) and, taking a line each, try reading the speech as described.

Differentiation
For older/more confident learners: Encourage the children to search through the book for other examples of the ways in which the characters speak.
For younger/less confident learners: Allow the children to select the three words they feel most able to broach (for example, 'shouted', 'commanded' and 'sobbed').

Planting vocabulary

Objective: To explore how writers use language for comic and dramatic effects.
What you need: Copies of *The Secret Garden*, a selection of different dictionaries.

What to do

● Children best develop vocabulary in speech before writing; this activity provides them with practice in this.
● Ask the children to work in groups of four. Invite them to select a chapter from *The Secret Garden* to work on. Tell them to go through their chapter carefully and to note down any vocabulary with which they are either unfamiliar with or only partly familiar with, for example, *astonished, tremulous* and *alighted*.
● Provide a range of dictionaries for the children to look up their words and tell them to discuss the definitions. Encourage them to consult at least two different dictionaries if possible.
● Ask the children to choose their five favourite words from the list and to have fun trying to think of things to say to each other using the words.
● Challenge the children to keep a conversation going by actually answering each other's points and still using the new words.
● Make sure everyone in the group has noted down the words and encourage the children to use the words in the coming days in the classroom.

Differentiation
For older/more confident learners: Encourage the children to work on using the words purposefully. Can they create an exchange between them that uses all the selected words? Ensure they write this down.
For younger/less confident learners: Let the children focus on only three or four words.

Talk about it

A bit o' Yorkshire

> **Objective:** To explore how word meanings change when used in different contexts.
> **What you need:** Copies of *The Secret Garden*.
> **Cross-curricular link:** Geography.

What to do

● As a class, reflect on dialect – either the local one, or any varied dialect that children in the class might know.

● If your class is a dialect-free zone, talk about words that their parents or grandparents might use, or dialects they've heard on the television. Jot down words from any of these dialects. If you are lucky then you might find you have different versions of words for the same word.

● Flick through *The Secret Garden* and find sections where the characters talk in dialect (Chapters 18 and 24 are good sources). Read the exchanges aloud (in your best Yorkshire accent). Discuss together what the characters are saying. Does everyone understand? Repeat with another couple of passages.

● Challenge the children to turn to their talk partner and try to have a conversation in the Yorkshire dialect (explain that the conversation can just be a typical social conversations they would normally have).

> **Differentiation**
> **For older/more confident learners:** Invite the children to investigate Yorkshire vocabulary and create a convincing dialogue to share with the class.
> **For younger/less confident learners:** Ask the children to focus on Dickon's lines at the opening of Chapter 22. Can they create a convincing version of Dickon speaking?

Talking to Mary

> **Objective:** To reflect on how working in role helps to explore complex issues.
> **What you need:** Copies of *The Secret Garden*.
> **Cross-curricular link:** PSHE.

What to do

● Ask the children to work in groups of four. Ensure that every child has a copy of the book.

● Ask the children to skim through the book on their own to find a point in the story when Mary faces a scary situation. For example, when she is listening to the screams of people with cholera; when she finds out everyone is dead or gone; when she arrives at the Manor; when she first hears Colin crying, and so on.

● Ask the children to share the situation with the rest of the group. Allow time for them to find a new situation if there is a duplication of events, so that each group has four situations to choose from.

● Now ask the children to role play a conversation between Mary and three other children immediately after each of these events. Each child in the group should have the opportunity to be Mary.

● Ask the children to imagine what Mary would say at each of these points. The child role-playing Mary should describe what has happened and how she feels after the event, and the other three children should react, asking questions and sympathising.

> **Differentiation**
> **For older/more confident learners:** Ask the children to write a conversation between Mary and a made-up character in one of the situations listed.
> **For younger/less confident learners:** Let the children focus only on one scene in the book.

Talk about it

A bit of earth

● Read through this script with your partner and discuss how to act it out.

Mr Craven: Are you well?

Mary: Yes.

Mr Craven: Do they take good care of you?

Mary: Yes.

(Mr Craven turns away from her)

Mr Craven: I forgot you. How could I remember you? I intended to send you a governess or nurse or someone of that sort, but I forgot.

Mary: *(Choking on the words)* Please… please…

Mr Craven: *(Facing her)* What do you want to say?

Mary: I am… I am too big for a nurse. And please – please don't make me have a governess yet.

Mr Craven: *(Absent-mindedly)* That was what the Sowerby woman said. *(Rousing himself)* What do you want to do?

Mary: *(Quavering)* Might I… might I have a bit of earth?

Mr Craven: Earth! What do you mean?

Mary: To plant seeds in – to make things grow – to see them come alive.

Mr Craven: *(Gazes at her)* A bit of earth. *(Passes a hand over his eyes)* You remind me of someone else who loved the earth and things that grow. When you see a bit of earth you want *(he smiles)*, take it, child, and make it come alive.

Mary: May I take it from anywhere – if it's not wanted?

Mr Craven: Anywhere. There! You must go now, I am tired.

Who said what?

- Who said these quotations? When and why did they say them?
- Discuss each quote in your group and then write your answers in the empty boxes.

	Who said it?	When?	Why?
'A more marred-looking young one I never saw in my life.' (Chapter 2)			
'I'm lonely.' (Chapter 4)			
'No wonder it is still... I am the first person who has spoken in here for ten years.' (Chapter 9)			
'Why does tha' care so much about roses an' such, all of a sudden?' (Chapter 10)			
'I'll plant them for thee myself. Where is tha' garden?' (Chapter 10)			
'May I take it from anywhere – if it's not wanted?' (Chapter 12)			

SECTION 5

Hysterical!

- Cut out these words and phrases and place them face down on the table.
- Take it in turns to turn over one card at a time.
- Try to say something in the style stated on your selected card.

almost shouted	gasped
sobbed	shouted
choked	contradicted fiercely
commanded	hesitated

Get writing

Mystery deviser

> **Objective:** To experiment with different narrative forms and styles to write their own stories.
> **What you need:** Photocopiable page 28.
> **Cross-curricular link:** Art.

What to do

● Discuss the mystery of the crying in the night and remind the children about its place in the story. (It adds to the early atmosphere at Misselthwaite Manor.) Ask: *What do we discover?* (That this is a sad shut-away child who, according to his uncle, is crippled.)

● Provide each child with photocopiable page 28. Explain to the children that they are going to use the ideas on the sheet to create their own mystery.

● Talk through the progress of the mystery: something mysterious happens; there are some clues; the mystery is solved; and an explanation is given.

● Ask the children to tick their preferred option at each stage and to use the planning space below to provide notes on how they will develop this part of the story.

● Explain that they need to choose the appropriate explanation to match their chosen mystery. For example, the person wandering around in the night could be looking for something stolen from them.

● Provide the children with time to write their mystery. The children will probably need an additional session to work on a polished written and illustrated mystery story.

> **Differentiation**
> **For older/more confident learners:** Encourage the children to work on a dramatic oral telling of their mystery story with sound effects.
> **For younger/less confident learners:** Allow the children to select from just two options per category/section.

Letters from Mary

> **Objective:** To reflect independently and critically on their own writing and edit and improve it.
> **What you need:** Copies of *The Secret Garden*, writing paper and envelopes.
> **Cross-curricular link:** History.

What to do

● Working in pairs, ask the children to imagine that Mary made friends on the ship with a child going to boarding school. Ask them to agree on a name for the child and to decide who will be Mary and who will be the friend.

● Ask the children playing the role of Mary to write a letter to her friend at boarding school just after she's arrived at the Manor, saying how strange and lonely it is. Mary should also ask a question or two of her friend.

● While the partner playing Mary is writing the letter, the other child should spend time developing their new character and the life they are living at boarding school.

● The boarding school friend should then reply to Mary, answering any questions, responding to Mary's story, providing advice and thinking of some story to tell about an event that took place at their Edwardian school.

● The letters can continue to be swapped (as enthusiasm allows) with one child unfolding the story of *The Secret Garden* and the other creating a boarding school story.

> **Differentiation**
> **For older/more confident learners:** Challenge the children to take on the unknown boarding school storyline.
> **For younger/less confident learners:** Ask the children to write short postcards from Mary.

Get writing

Character change

> **Objective:** To set their own challenges to extend achievement and experience in writing.
> **What you need:** Copies of *The Secret Garden*, photocopiable page 29, scissors, paper and glue.
> **Cross-curricular link:** History.

What to do

- Discuss how the characters of Mary and Colin change (they become interested in life; they care for others; they become healthy), and why (people expect them to behave well; they hear about things that interest them; they take outdoor exercise; they meet other children).
- Invite the class to write a story about a flawed person who changes.
- Provide each child with photocopiable page 29. Ask the children to think of ideas for each of the ten prompts listed and make notes. For example, who the character might have been mean to and why; who they met and where; what mistake they made and what the consequence was.

- Invite the children to invent a character and decide how they are flawed. Which of their ideas works best with this character?
- Ask the children to select and cut out six prompts and to stick them onto a new piece of paper in their desired order. They should annotate details around each one to create a story plan. For example: rich character who is mean to a beggar; loses money; meets another beggar; helps this beggar, receives gift from beggar who is really rich.
- Provide time for them to develop their story.

> **Differentiation**
> **For older/more confident learners:** Challenge the children to write a story where the reader really engages with the main character's progress.
> **For younger/less confident learners:** Allow the children to choose just two elements to work with; support them to develop a character and to understand how they change.

Nature notebook

> **Objective:** To adapt non-narrative forms and styles to write fiction or factual texts, including poems.
> **What you need:** Copies of *The Secret Garden*, individual notebooks and pencils.
> **Cross-curricular link:** Science.

What to do

- Explain to the children that in this activity they will create nature diaries as a preparation for report writing.
- First, skim through *The Secret Garden* with the children, noting Mary's gradual appreciation of nature and the outdoors.
- If possible, look at examples of nature notebooks, such as *The Country Diary of an Edwardian Lady* by Edith Holden.
- Provide the children with individual notebooks and take a walk through the local area, identifying

trees and collecting leaves. Take leaf rubbings and sketch acorns and chestnut cases and so on. Ask the children to sketch any wildlife that they observe (including minibeasts), writing brief descriptions of how they move and where they were found.

- In another session, ask the children to compile an illustrated report about their nature walk, capturing the main events that take place at that particular time of the year. Encourage the use of descriptive language.

> **Differentiation**
> **For older/more confident learners:** Encourage the children to maintain their nature notebook over at least one school term.
> **For younger/less confident learners:** Allow the children to focus on one or two selected areas (animals or plants) for report writing.

Get writing

Stately manor

> **Objective:** To experiment with different narrative form and styles to write their own stories.
> **What you need:** Copies of *The Secret Garden*, paper and photocopiable page 30.
> **Cross-curricular link:** Geography.

What to do
● Make an A3 copy of the map on photocopiable page 30. (You could soak it in tea and dry it in the oven to create the appearance of an old document.)
● Working in groups of six, ask the children to look at the map and to imagine that they are somewhere on the old estate. Where would they explore?
● Encourage them to think imaginatively about the map as a story setting and share their ideas. Ask: *Which locations sound like the sorts of places where stories occur? What might have happened in the past here? What could have been lost in the pond? Who may have lived in the old ruined keeper's lodge?*
● Following the group discussions, provide each child with photocopiable page 30. Ask them to annotate the map with their favourite story ideas for several of the locations.
● Provide time for the children to plan an extended story and write a central scene (for example, finding something in the pond, or the railway bridge collapsing).

> **Differentiation**
> **For older/more confident learners:** Ask the children to add two new locations and story ideas to the map.
> **For younger/less confident learners:** Allow the children to focus on a selected trio of locations between which the story takes place.

Mother stories

> **Objective:** To create multi-layered texts, including use of hyperlinks and linked web pages.
> **What you need:** Copies of *The Secret Garden* and access to computers.
> **Cross-curricular link:** PSHE.

What to do
● Together, focus on the three mothers in *The Secret Garden*: Mrs Lennox, Mrs Craven and Mrs Sowerby. Compare how they are represented as mothers.
● Ask the children to choose one of these women and create an imaginary biography for her. Bring out Mrs Lennox's passion for parties (but not children), Mrs Craven's love of gardens (and possible potential as a mother) or Mrs Sowerby's love of her children and her wisdom. Help the children to create their biographies as linked web pages if possible.
● Discuss other stories involving mother characters (Jacqueline Wilson has some great examples). Let the children interview willing staff members about their mothers, and encourage them to talk to the women in their own families.
● Ask the children to write a biography of their mother/guardian or one of the mothers they've heard about. Encourage them to embellish the text with photos, captions, video and audio files. They might also like to create anecdotes in 'case history' type boxes. Link all the biographies together as a series of web pages.
● When the biographies are complete, invite parents into the school to attend a launch of the Mum's Collection on screen or in print.

> **Differentiation**
> **For older/more confident learners:** Challenge the children to produce short biographies about other people of their choice.
> **For younger/less confident learners:** Ask the children to simply record a couple of anecdotes about their own mothers.

Mystery deviser

- Use the ideas on this planner to devise a mystery in which you encounter and solve strange goings-on at an old manor. Think of what is hidden and work backwards to devise three clues. Tick your selections.

Mysterious occurrence	Clues	How the mystery is solved	Explanation
I heard a strange noise in the night. ☐	I found the remains of a note in the fireplace. ☐	I hid and observed things going on. ☐	Someone had stolen something. ☐
I saw someone wandering near the house at night. ☐	I heard one of the servants say something by mistake. ☐	I confronted someone and asked them a question. ☐	Everyone in the house was keeping a secret about one resident. ☐
I was told something special was missing. ☐	One night, I looked out of my window and saw something. ☐	I followed somebody. ☐	Someone had done something wrong and it needed resolving. ☐
Details:	Details:	Details:	Details:

Character change

● Use the prompts below to plan a story in which a character changes.

was mean to	met
lost	fell in love with
helped	fell out with
made the mistake of	found
realised	wrote a letter to

Stately manor

- Examine this map and in selected locations annotate it with your favourite story ideas.

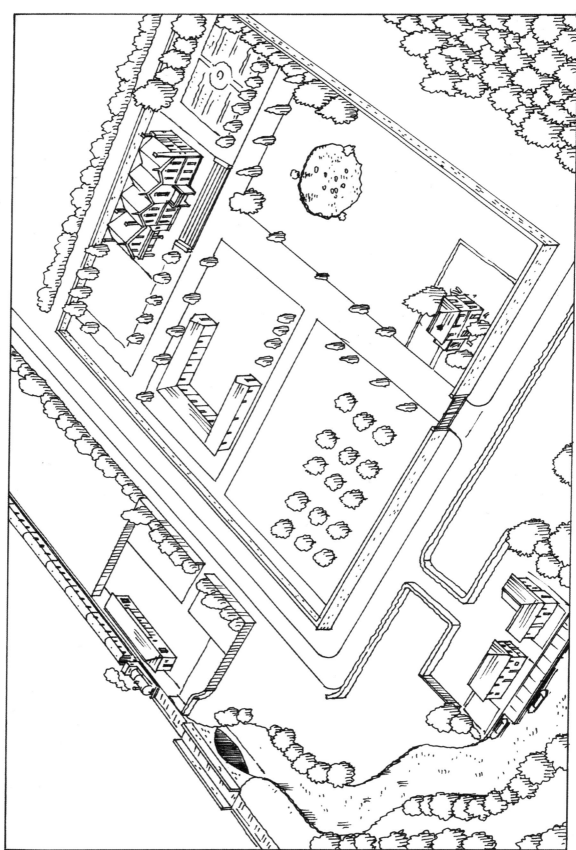

Illustration © 2011, Jon Mitchell (Beehive Illustration).

Assessment

Assessment advice

Not much happens in *The Secret Garden* event-wise – it's all about character and personal growth. As the children work through the book, assess their ability to see the changes in the characters, particularly in the characters of Mary and Colin. Using pegging cards on two lines across the room, build up a progression of Mary and Colin's characters as they change through the story.

The story outlined in *The Secret Garden* is an excellent basis for a discussion about the reader's feelings towards a character. It is not often that the children will have had the experience of being introduced to main characters in a book with such unattractive personalities. Gauge the children's feelings towards different characters half way through the book. Invite them to discuss both the character and their changing feelings towards that person. Many crucial changes happen in the middle of the book, then play themselves out. For example, by the time Colin has his row with Mary the story is then unfolded and just progresses. Can the children link an event such as this to a change in Mary or Colin? Peg pivotal events to character changes already pegged to the line.

Finally, focus the children's attention once more on the character changes that take place between the beginning and the end of the book. Encourage the children to explore some of the minor characters, such as Mr Craven and Mrs Medlock. Can they see how these characters change too?

People change

> **Assessment focus:** To deduce, infer or interpret information, events or ideas from the text.
> **What you need:** Photocopiable page 32.

What to do
● The relationships between different people in *The Secret Garden* is one of the key ways in which Frances Hodgson Burnett demonstrates character (and how it can change).

● Photocopiable page 32 can be used to help the children explore how characters in the book feel about each other at different stages of the story. You can repeat the activity outlined below at appropriate key points in the book.

● Provide each child with photocopiable page 32. Tell them to pick one name from each box at the top of the sheet (two different names). Then ask them to use their two selected characters to answer the two questions. (For each question, the children should write the first name in the first empty space and the second name in the second space.)

● Some combinations of characters require more imagination from the children but they can highlight some interesting features of the story that lend themselves to further exploration. For example, can we assume that Ben likes Dickon? Allow the children the opportunity to investigate these relationships with a free hand.

● If there is sufficient time, encourage the children to repeat the activity, this time selecting different characters.

People change

● Choose a name from each of the two boxes, then answer the questions below.

Mrs Medlock, Colin, Mary, Ben

Mrs Medlock, Martha, Dickon, Mary

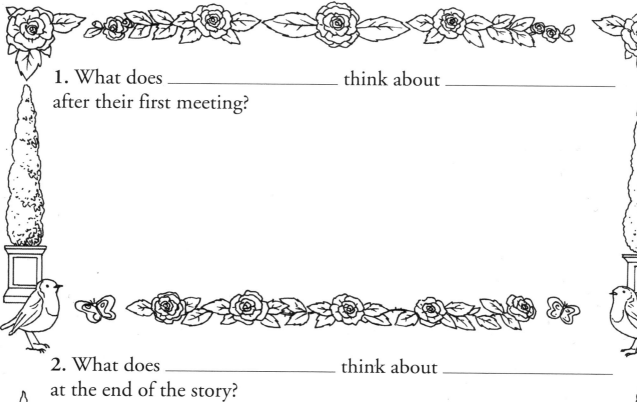

1. What does _____ think about _____ after their first meeting?

2. What does _____ think about _____ at the end of the story?

READ & RESPOND: Activities based on The Secret Garden

SCHOLASTIC
www.scholastic.co.uk

Illustration © 2011, Jon Mitchell (Beehive Illustration).